HOW TO HEAL
FROM HEARTBREAK
(or at least feel less broken)

HOW TO HEAL FROM HEARTBREAK

(or at least feel less broken)

A BREAKUP JOURNAL

carissa potter & vera kachouh

A TARCHERPERIGEE BOOK

tarcherperigee

an imprint of Penguin Random House LLC
penguinrandomhouse.com

Most TarcherPerigee books are available at special quantity discounts for bulk
purchase for sales promotions, premiums, fund-raising, and educational needs.
Special books or book excerpts also can be created to fit specific needs. For
details, write: SpecialMarkets@penguinrandomhouse.com.

Library of Congress Control Number: 2022934847

ISBN (trade paperback) 9780593541104

Printed in the United States of America
1st Printing

Book design by Shannon Nicole Plunkett

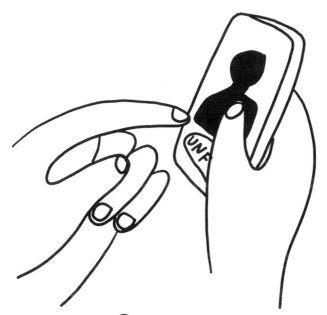

SOMETIMES
IT'S BETTER <u>NOT</u>
KNOWING...

THIS BOOK
BELONGS TO:

_____

_____

It's a record of
the transformative
power of grief &
all the messy/
beautiful feelings
that come with
the human
experience of love.

A DEDICATION TO
YOUR HEARTBROKEN SELF

WRITE DOWN ALL THE THINGS
YOU NEED TO HEAR RIGHT NOW.

dear heartbroken self,
you are the most wonderful,
kind human & i love you...

Dear Heartbroken Reader,

We're writing to you from the other side (sort of). If you're here, you might be wondering: How will I ever get over this? Will I ever feel better? Well . . . it's going to be a while. But sadness, like the weather, does eventually change, even if our moods don't believe in each other.*

And anyway, who can predict the future?

At the beginning of a breakup, you will experience a tumult of emotions: shock, disbelief, pain, relief, exaltation, and/or sadness, to name a few. Friends and family want you to move past your pain. Maybe even to "get over it." But that's just not how your brain works.†

(this is also frightening)

Studies suggest that emotional pain activates the same receptors in our brain as physical pain. That's why "get over it" is not a reasonable strategy. Because you actually hurt. A lot.

Maybe you feel like your chest is compressing. Maybe you feel like your throat has a knot in it or your hands tingle whenever you think about the breakup. We've felt, at times, like we're literally drowning. Waves of sadness creep up and threaten to pin you under the tide.

---

* Emerson said this.

† We're definitely not neuroscientists.

This book is the life raft.

Or maybe let's just say this book is *one* of the life rafts (there are plenty more inside this book to choose from).

We are two friends who have held hands through many heartbreaks, and we wrote the book we wish we'd had. We wrote the book we needed when our friends just got tired of hearing about it (again and again).

help with holding on to & making sense of it all.

So, what is this book?

It's a judgment-free place to put the pain of breaking up. It's a 240-page acknowledgment that your grief and your experiences are real. If you use it actively—and we hope you do!—it will become a record of this time in your life that you can look back on once the clouds have shifted. You can thumb through the pages and think: *WHOA, I made it through some tough shit. I am FREAKING AMAZING.* Because really, you are.

All you need is a pen or pencil. You already know the way.

With all our (hopelessly broken,* endlessly romantic, stupid deadbeat) hearts,

VERA & CARISSA

---

* Somewhat less

HOW TO USE THIS JOURNAL

We designed this journal based on the emotional experience of breaking up and feeling heartbreak. Which means that you can stop and start anywhere you want. Because grief usually looks like this:

And not (regrettably) like this:

We offer a beginning, a few middles, and a (somewhat) end as a way to guide you through the pain. But sometimes shock (our beginning) doesn't come until the middle, and sometimes getting by (our end) is really only the beginning. Make your own path. Do the book twice. There is no wrong way through the pain. Just keep moving.

A few essentials to have on hand:

1. Pen or pencil
2. Maybe something cozy
3. Your good-for-nothing (but holding out for hope) broken heart

HOW TO HEAL FROM HEARTBREAK

(or at least feel less broken)

EMOTIONAL
CHECK-IN
check all the feels going
on inside right now...

- ☐ SHOCK
- ☐ HOPE
- ☐ RAGE
- ☐ SADNESS
- ☐ RESENTMENT
- ☐ RELIEF
- ☐ HUNGER
- ☐ NUMBNESS
- ☐ EMPTINESS
- ☐ EXHAUSTION
- ☐ JEALOUSY
- ☐ GRUMPINESS
- ☐ APATHY
- ☐ _____
- ☐ _____
- ☐ _____

POSSIBLE ACTIONS TO FOCUS ON

- ☐ PUT ONE FOOT IN FRONT OF THE OTHER
- ☐ FUCK MAKING YOUR BED, JUST GET OUT OF IT IF YOU CAN
- ☐ GET DRESSED (SOMETIMES PAJAMAS ARE OKAY TOO)
- ☐ CONNECT WITH FRIENDS
- ☐ GET OUT OF YOUR HEAD
- ☐ LET'S BE HONEST, MAYBE MAKE OUT WITH SOMEONE?
- ☐ _____
  _____
- ☐ _____
  _____

FACETIME WITH FRIENDS

THE BEGINNING...*

SHOCK
a fresh cut
a new wound

STUDIES SUGGEST THAT
EMOTIONAL PAIN ACTIVATES
THE SAME RECEPTORS IN OUR
BRAINS AS PHYSICAL PAIN

(or to put it another way:
You're NOT crazy. It
actually hurts.)

*GRIEF DOESN'T HAVE A
TIMELINE, BUT YOU HAVE
TO START SOMEWHERE

BREAKUP CHECKLIST

- ☐ UNFOLLOW YOUR EX (srsly)
- ☐ GET RID OF THEIR STUFF (or sell it and keep the $, It feels good)
- ☐ CLEAN YOUR SPACE
- ☐ MUTE ANY MUTUAL FRIENDS ON SOCIAL MEDIA WHO MIGHT POST PICS
- ☐
- ☐
- ☐
- ☐
- ☐
- ☐

(add your list of personalized rituals to help you keep some space.)

THINGS THAT REMIND ME OF YOU

ME OF YOU

why does
everyone in the
world drive the same
car as you now???

THINGS YOU'RE NEVER GETTING BACK

that super
soft tee of
yours i wear
every day

SIRI, CALL...

LIST THE PEOPLE YOU CAN
CALL WHO WON'T JUDGE YOU
AND WON'T TRY TO FIX YOU.

do you
remember
anyone's
phone
number?

PHONE
BOOK

867 5309

~~555-5555~~

COMPLETE THIS THOUGHT

ALL THROUGHOUT OUR
RELATIONSHIP, I WAS
SO SCARED THAT...

(i'd
spill &
make
a
mess
of
us.)

EMOTIONS AS DATA

THINK OF EMOTIONS AS DATA.
RECORD WHAT YOU'RE FEELING
FOR ONE WEEK.

(MON:)

(TUES:)

(WEDS:)

(THURS:)

FRI:

SAT:

SUN:

WHAT HAVE YOU LEARNED?

WHAT HAS CHANGED?

CONCRETE PLANS

WHO CAN I ASK TO CHECK IN ON ME EVERY DAY?

NAME 4 PEOPLE WHO MAKE YOU FEEL GOOD:

1.   3.

2.   4.

LIST 4 ACTIVITIES YOU'VE BEEN WANTING TO TRY:

1.   3.

2.   4.

NOW MATCH THE PEOPLE WITH THE ACTIVITES:*

1. I THINK_____
   SHOULD DO_____

2. I THINK I'LL ASK_____
   TO DO_____

3. I THINK_____
   WILL ENJOY_____

4. I WANT TO DO_____
   WITH_____

REACH OUT!!!

*DOING NEW THINGS TOGETHER
 BONDS US & MAKES US FEEL
 CONNECTED

SCHEDULE IT!!!*

M	T	W	TH	F	SAT	SUN

*Studies show it helps to schedule stuff

<u>MAKE A DETAILED PLAN</u>
<u>OF</u> <u>ONE</u> <u>WEEK</u>*

MONDAY

TUESDAY

WEDNESDAY

THURSDAY

FRIDAY

SATURDAY

SUNDAY

* add 1 fun thing each day

THINGS TO LOOK FORWARD TO

WHO AM I NOW?

(ME BEFORE)

wanted to be:

loved doing:

never forgot to:

(ME AFTER)

wants to be:

loves doing:

never forgets to:

LOCATE YOUR HEARTBREAK IN YOUR BODY

MARK ANY TENSE SPOTS,
POINTS OF JOY,
ACHES, CRAVINGS,
CRAMPS,
TENDERNESS,
OR WHATEVER
GRABS YOU.

DESCRIBE WHERE IT HURTS

AFTER A BREAKUP, PEOPLE
REPORT PHYSICAL SENSATIONS
THAT ARE SIMILAR TO GRIEVING
THE DEATH OF A LOVED ONE:
- Chest pressure
- Tightness in the throat
- A feeling of drowning
- Tingling in the limbs
- Waves of sadness rolling in
  and out like the tide

PLACE YOUR
HAND OVER THE
PAIN & JUST HOLD IT.

EYES: CONFUSION, WANTING TO SEE & BE SEEN

HEAD: ANXIETY, LACK OF TRUST IN PROCESS OF LIFE

JAW: TENSION, RAGE, ANGER

HEART: WHERE JOY & LOVE ARE

NUMB ARMS: LACK OF CONTROL, WANTING AGENCY

GUT: BASICALLY THIS COULD BE ANYTHING & EVERYTHING

HANDS: PROBLEMS LETTING GO

LEGS: WORRY ABOUT THE FUTURE, INSTABILITY

FEET: FEELING DISCONNECTED, LOST, OR WITHOUT PURPOSE

LIST SOME MOVIES
THAT GIVE YOU HOPE

OURS:
- MOONSTRUCK
- FRENCH KISS
- ABOUT TIME
- LOVE ACTUALLY
- SHAKESPEARE
  IN LOVE

LIST SOME MOVIES THAT HELP YOU WALLOW

OURS:
- MOONLIGHT
- BLUE IS THE WARMEST COLOR
- THE FAULT IN OUR STARS
- 500 DAYS OF SUMMER
- CALL ME BY YOUR NAME
- THE BODYGARD

MOVIE NIGHT IS A GREAT EXCUSE TO HAVE POPCORN FOR DINNER

a complete meal*

* said no health experts ever. but whatever.

Topping ideas: Parmesan & black pepper, za'atar & olive oil, togarashi & honey powder

<u>PERMISSION</u> TO <u>EAT</u>
<u>YOUR</u> <u>HEART</u> <u>OUT</u>

LIST 5 THINGS YOU ARE
CRAVING RIGHT NOW:

1.

2.

3.

4.

5.

LONGING VS. HATE

PLACE YOURSELF ON THE SPECTRUM
OF LONGING & HATRED FOR 1 WEEK

HATE →

all the feelings in between

LONGING ←

DAY 1   DAY 2   DAY 3

CONNECT THE DOTS TO VISUALIZE
YOUR EMOTIONAL WAVES

DAY 4   DAY 5   DAY 6   DAY 7

<u>RELISH</u> <u>YOUR</u> <u>RAGE</u>

ANGER CAN BE A HELPFUL EMOTION.
DIG INTO IT & WRITE DOWN WHAT COMES
UP FOR YOU ON THIS PAGE.

VENTING OFTEN MAKES THE FEELING
STRONGER, BUT IT CAN ALSO HELP YOU
SEE THE REASONS THINGS JUST WEREN'T
WORKING.

NOW, MAKE SOMETHING BEAUTIFUL WITH YOUR RAGE

- PUT ICE IN A PLASTIC BAG
- BASH IT WITH A ROLLING PIN
- PUT THE CRUSHED ICE ON A PLATE
- ARRANGE FRUIT ON TOP
- RELISH THE SWEETNESS

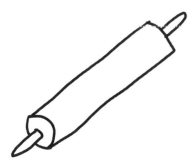

DO 1 NICE THING FOR YOURSELF TODAY*

breathe extra deeply

nice things i could do for myself

buy fresh flowers

order takeout

TODAY I WILL

_____

*IT CAN BE SUPER SIMPLE

RESEARCH DIFFERENT TYPES OF THERAPY

IF A PRACTICE SEEMS LIKE A GOOD FIT, TRY IT.

OK. JUST SO WE'RE CLEAR, YOU LOVE ME SO MUCH YOU WANT TO SEE OTHER PEOPLE?

Interlude

SOME OF THE MOST EMBARRASSING BREAK-UP STORIES FROM PEOPLE WHO HAVE BEEN THERE

BREAKUPS CAN FEEL SUPER ISOLATING. TAKE COMFORT IN THE PAIN OF OTHERS.

My boyfriend was coming over and I decided to put on something sexy. (Oh, to be twenty-four and in love . . .) When I answered the door, he was Eeyore-level forlorn and sat me down to tell me it was over. I was still wearing the sexy outfit and was completely shocked. I didn't see it coming at all. Getting dumped is rough at the best of times, but I was wearing tiny, sheer lingerie and weeping uncontrollably so I felt completely ridiculous as well as heartbroken. In the weeks after the split, I went on to make questionable choices, like leaving mementos from when we were together on the hood of his car while he was at work. That said, I don't know if anything tops the actual breakup.

* ❋ ❋

We broke up over the phone while I was sitting in the bedroom at an annual party—the same party we had met at exactly one year earlier—so all of our mutual friends were aware that this was happening. Also, it happened to be my birthday.

❋ ❋ *

I thought I saw my ex on the street (I saw him *everywhere* in those early post-breakup days). I panicked and backed my truck into a median on a crowded street. Luckily, no one got hurt, and I didn't even get a ticket.

I was really, really lonely and young when I met X. He and I didn't live in the same place and neither of us had the money it takes to keep up a long-distance relationship. But we were both lonely enough that summer, I think, to try something pretty doomed from the start. For a little while it was so soft and nice, lots of long phone conversations and a few emotionally charged long weekends. But by early winter, he became less lonely than I was and decided we should stop talking to each other. A healthy person would have probably nursed her heartbreak for a little while then moved on, but I was so, so sad, and like a lot of people heartbroken in the age of social media, I checked his Facebook page often for "clues" that he might be thinking about me as much as I was thinking about him.

At some point around then, the layout of Facebook changed, and the "make a post" box went right up to the top, where the search bar had been. One day, I went to type X's full name into the search bar, which is how I always pulled up his page, and just after I hit enter, a friend stopped by and I walked away from my computer without finishing my usual scrutinizing.

A day or so later a different friend asked me if I'd meant to make a post that was just two words: X's first and last name. When I checked my page, there it was: X's full name, typed out in front of everyone, up for at least a day. Mortification doesn't even begin to describe how I felt, and I deleted my whole profile not long after that.

✳ ✺ ✳

A guy who really put me through the wringer finally broke up with me after creating prolonged emotional chaos. I was so angry that in the heat of the moment, I punched him in the shoulder. Because I don't know how to land a punch, two things happened: he was absolutely fine and I broke a bone in my hand.

✻ ✺ ✻

I got engaged to my partner after several years of being together, and we had begun the process of telling our friends and family, setting the date, making arrangements, etc. Over the course of the months between getting engaged and the actual date, my partner began to have doubts and, ultimately, he decided that he wasn't ready to commit. We broke up, he moved out, our engagement was off. It was so humiliating to tell everyone it wasn't going to happen. It's one of those things you see in movies but never think will happen to you: the cold-feet situation, the called-off wedding. I was thankful it didn't happen on the actual wedding day but it was still such a humiliating experience and it totally destroyed any fantasies I may have had about what it would be like when I get married. Not the dream scenario I was picturing, to say the least.

✺ ✻ ✺

He said, "It's been nice talking to you." What??? We did more than that.

✻ ✺ ✻

He told me, "We weren't really, like, *together* together." But a few weeks before, he had said we should have babies together. (!!!)

✺ ✻ ✺

He broke up with me in front of his parents because he was "embarrassed by my body."

* * *

Let me set the stage, because there was literally a stage involved. It was the spring of 1989 at the Miss Summerland Blossom Pageant and I was vying for the title of Blossom Queen. (Please don't judge me, it was a different time.) My high school sweetheart was going to be my escort for the big night. We'd been together since the ninth grade and here I was at the end of my junior year. In love? Oh yes. Madly. Well, we *were* madly in love until I found out he was cheating on me! I dumped him through a river of my own, absolutely betrayed, sixteen-year-old tears.

Unfortunately, the pageant was only a few days away, and there wasn't time to find another date who knew the choreography required to get each girl onstage. (Again, it was a different time!) Now this is where things get embarrassing. Our small-town theater was packed and, as in most small towns, everyone knew everything about everyone, including the sordid details about my broken heart. Anyway, it was finally my turn to walk on stage. And, as was expected, we had to walk arm-in-arm to center stage, where I would then curtsy to the outgoing Queen—who happened to be the girl he was caught making out with!

Wait! You probably want to know if the night was saved, and if the ultimate revenge was mine. Nope. I lost Blossom Queen.

* * *

We broke up at a cat video festival and instead of leaving, I stayed through the whole thing, sobbing and laughing because some videos were just too funny.

***

We only dated for six months...and potentially that's why it stung like it did. I was still in the honeymoon phase, and he was, well...on tour with his band. He wrote me love letters from the road. But then, the letters slowed down. Finally, he broke things off. I begged him to reconsider. I told him it wasn't just simply *his* choice to make.

Then the email came in about how we'd fallen out of touch and how he'd found someone new. It ended like this: "This is from someone who loved you much, cares for you still, and will honor you always."

Of course, one might think, "Awwwww, he will honor you always!" But all I could focus on was the new girl. My heart sank. I lied to him and told him I was also seeing someone new. He met her when he was with me. Did he cheat? I will never know. But he fell out of love with me, so the outcome ultimately was still shit.

Writing this, a part of me misses him. I wish I could text him and say, "Hey, I learned a lot from us. I forgive you." But I will never text him.

***

It was the summer of 1975—I was dating a gal from my hometown of Willmar, central Minnesota, who was a student at Montana State University. I was really smitten with her, as she embodied everything I was attracted to in a girl. One of the things about her that I found attractive was that she was a thrill seeker (skydiver, etc.). The previous school year, I had attended a University of Minnesota skydiving meeting and found it all extremely enticing/compelling, but I couldn't imagine myself jumping out of an airplane. That fall, she went back to school (in Montana) and, unbeknownst to me, to her boyfriend. I was devastated and totally dysfunctional as a result. I was at a loss as to what to do to get myself out of my funk. Then it dawned on me—I would go skydiving. Just one problem—I didn't have any money. So I went to the student loan department and told them that I needed an emergency loan to hold me over to buy groceries and other essentials until my student loan came through. I took the $150 loan and went to a local drop zone and, with tremendous trepidation, made my first skydive. Needless to say, it was exhilarating and just what the doctor ordered. I was instantly jolted from my intense, painful self-pity and was able to get on with my life, eventually making 175 skydives (not that many in the skydiving community) before settling down to raise kids.

—from Carissa's dad

THINGS COULD HAVE BEEN DIFFERENT...

BUT WHO KNOWS IF THEY WOULD HAVE BEEN BETTER?

THE MIDDLE*

MAKING
SENSE
OF
IT ALL
(OR AT LEAST A FEW THINGS)

* THERE IS NO EXACT MIDDLE, YOU
ARE JUST MOVING THROUGH LIFE
AT WHATEVER PACE FEELS RIGHT

EMOTIONAL
CHECK-IN
check all the feels going
on inside right now...

- ☐ SHOCK
- ☐ HOPE
- ☐ RAGE
- ☐ SADNESS
- ☐ RESENTMENT
- ☐ RELIEF
- ☐ HUNGER
- ☐ NUMBNESS
- ☐ EMPTINESS
- ☐ EXHAUSTION
- ☐ JEALOUSY
- ☐ GRUMPINESS
- ☐ APATHY
- ☐ _____
- ☐ _____
- ☐ _____

POSSIBLE ACTIONS TO FOCUS ON

- ☐ PUT ONE FOOT IN FRONT OF THE OTHER
- ☐ FUCK MAKING YOUR BED, JUST GET OUT OF IT IF YOU CAN
- ☐ GET DRESSED (SOMETIMES PAJAMAS ARE OKAY TOO)
- ☐ CONNECT WITH FRIENDS
- ☐ GET OUT OF YOUR HEAD
- ☐ LET'S BE HONEST, MAYBE MAKE OUT WITH SOMEONE?

- ☐ _____
  _____
  _____
- ☐ _____
  _____
  _____

LOCATE YOUR HEARTBREAK IN YOUR BODY

MARK ANY TENSE SPOTS,
POINTS OF JOY,
ACHES, CRAVINGS,
CRAMPS,
TENDERNESS,
OR WHATEVER
GRABS YOU.

PEOPLE & HANDS CHANGE
THROUGHOUT OUR LIVES.
USE YOUR PALM TO GAIN
INSIGHT.

HEART LINE:
ROMANCE, SEX,
COMMITMENT

HEAD LINE:
INTELLECTUAL PURSUITS

LIFE
LINE:
YOUR
LIFE
EXPERIENCE

FATE
LINE:
THINGS
OUTSIDE
YOUR
CONTROL

WHICH LINE IS THE STRONGEST?

ARE THERE BREAKS IN ANY LINES?

DO THE LINES WAVE OR ARE THEY STRAIGHT?

WHAT CAN YOU INTUIT FROM YOUR PALMS RIGHT NOW?

SPACE SURVEY

LOOK AROUND THE ROOM
YOU'RE IN. FIND AN OBJECT
THAT MAKES YOU FEEL LOVED.
DRAW IT BELOW.

NOW, WHAT IS THE STORY
BEHIND THAT OBJECT?

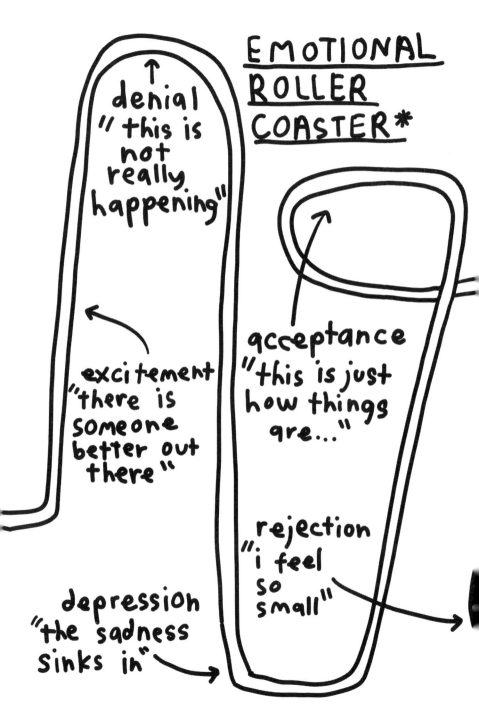

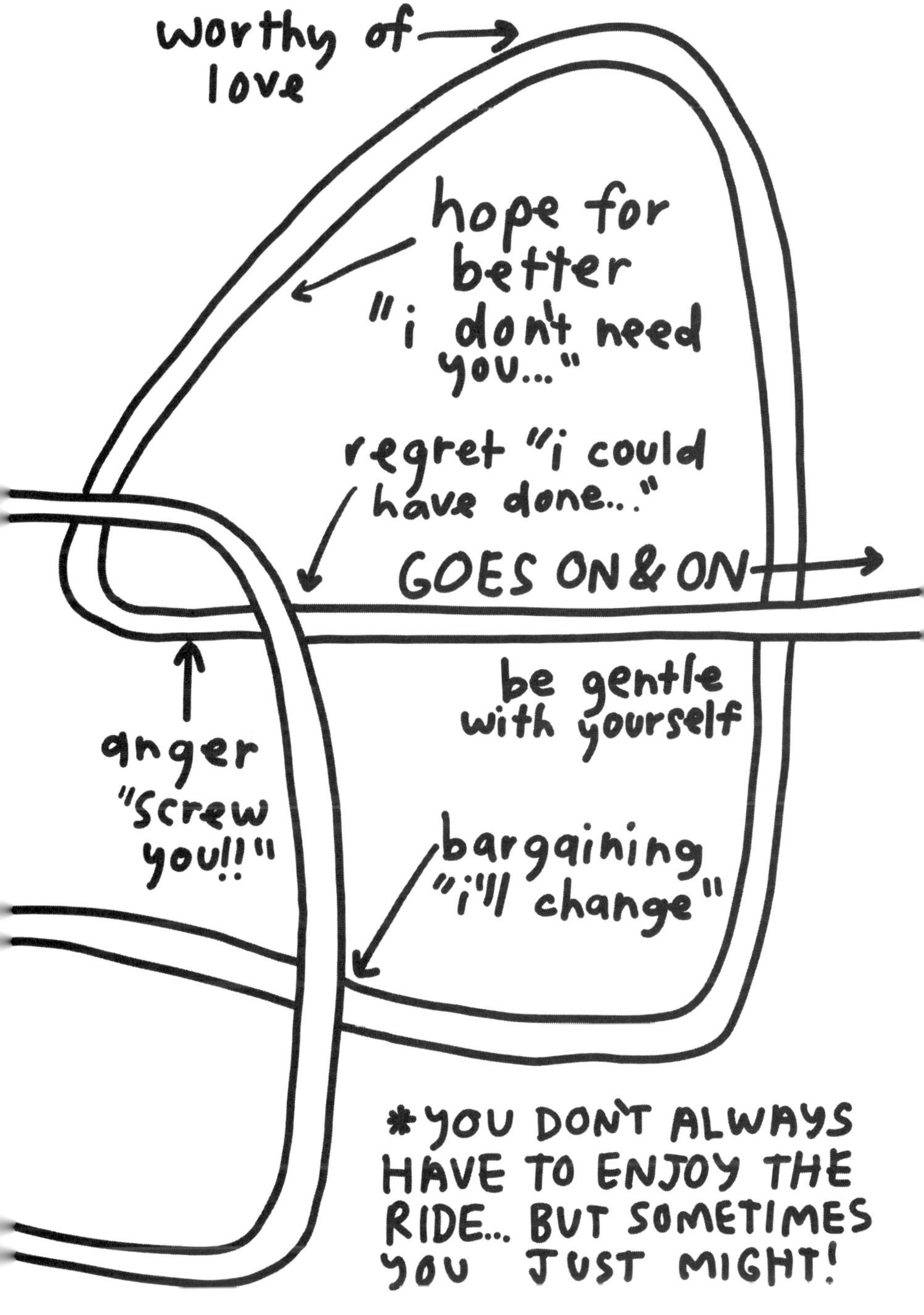
worthy of love
hope for better "i don't need you..."
regret "i could have done..."
GOES ON & ON
be gentle with yourself
anger "screw you!!"
bargaining "i'll change"
*YOU DON'T ALWAYS HAVE TO ENJOY THE RIDE... BUT SOMETIMES YOU JUST MIGHT!

EMOTIONAL ROLLER COASTER

PLOT SOME POINTS
ON YOUR OWN
EMOTIONAL ROLLER COASTER.

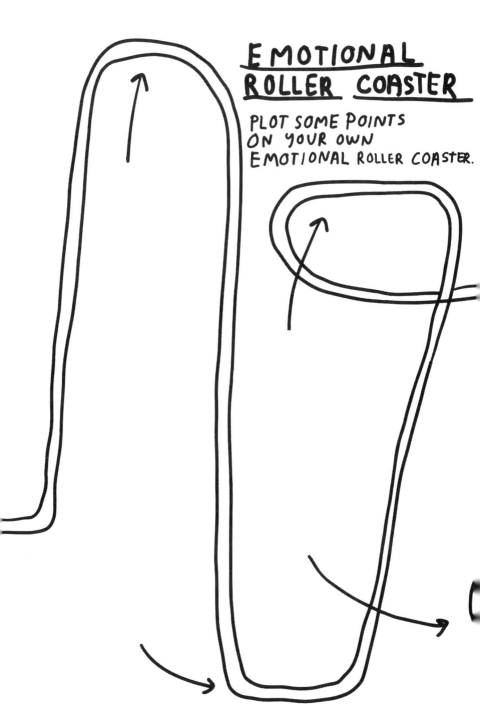

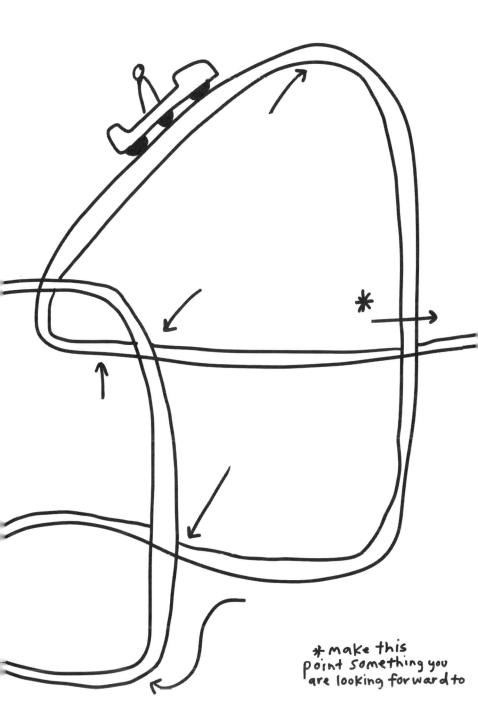

* make this
point something you
are looking forward to

WHAT WAS THE WORST FIGHT YOU EVER HAD? OR WHAT ARGUMENT DID YOU HAVE OVER & OVER?

WHAT DO YOU THINK THAT SAYS ABOUT YOUR RELATIONSHIP?

YOU DO
SOMETHING

YOU GET
HURT

I GET HURT

I DO
SOMETHING

GET OUT OF YOUR HEAD
BY OBSERVING THE WORLD

A POET ONCE SAID THAT ANYONE
CAN BE A WRITER IF THEY DO
THIS EVERYDAY:
NOTICE 6 ORDINARY THINGS &
WRITE THEM DOWN IN GREAT DETAIL.

1.

2.

3.

4.

5.

6.

WHO AM I NOW?

(ME BEFORE)

defined love as:

deal breakers:

looked for:

(ME AFTER)

defines love as:

deal breakers:

looking for:

WHERE & WHEN DID YOU MEET?

HOW DID IT FEEL IN YOUR BODY?

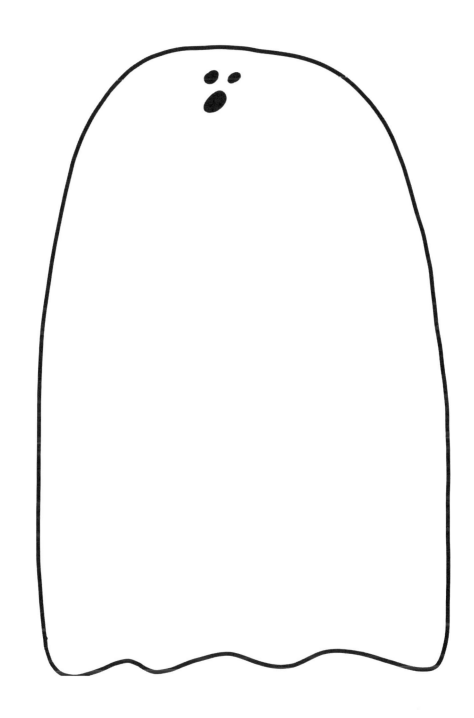

THINGS I MISS ABOUT THEM

THINGS I DON'T MISS ONE BIT

WHAT DO YOU THINK HEALING
SHOULD LOOK LIKE VS. WHAT
IT ACTUALLY LOOKS LIKE?

THIS MAY NOT FEEL LIKE HEALING,

BUT IT IS.

WRITE A LETTER YOU WILL NEVER SEND

dear jerkface,

ATTACHMENT STYLE

ATTACHMENT IS HOW YOU RELATE TO OTHER HUMANS; YOUR ATTACHMENT STYLE USUALLY DEVELOPS IN YOUTH.

ARE YOU:
- ☐ SECURE
- ☐ ANXIOUS
- ☐ AVOIDANT

WHY DO YOU THINK THIS IS YOUR STYLE?

Attachment theory was developed by psychologists Mary Ainsworth & John Bowlby in the 1950s. Turn to the back of the book for further reading, including the book ATTACHED.

HOW HAS THIS AFFECTED YOUR RELATIONSHIPS?

ALL THE THINGS I WISH THEY DID DIFFERENTLY

ALL THE THINGS I WISH I DID DIFFERENTLY

FOODS TO ILLUSTRATE MOODS

GATHER ONE OF EACH:
SPICY, SALTY, SWEET, SOUR.
TASTE THEM ONE BY ONE,
FOCUSING ON HOW EACH ONE
MAKES YOU FEEL.

WHAT DO YOUR TASTE BUDS
  WANT RIGHT NOW?

WHAT DOES YOUR HEART
WANT RIGHT NOW?

VISIT
HOWTOHEALFROMHEARTBREAK.COM
FOR RECIPE IDEAS.

YOU HAVE MADE IT THROUGH SOME TOUGH SHIT...

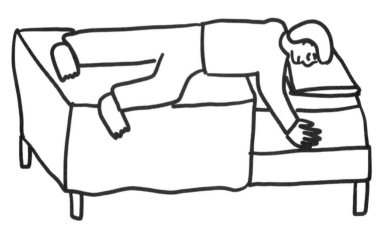

GIVE YOURSELF A BREAK.

BEING SINGLE IS...

~~HORRIBLE~~

~~AWESOME~~

BOTH?

STORIES OF JOY & GLOOM
(MOSTLY JOY)
FROM A FEW PEOPLE
WHO HAVE BEEN THERE

I love finding out how strong I am and how much I actually love being with myself!

* ** *

Single people have better sex.

* ** *

I was effectively single for seven years and that time helped me better understand what I love about my life without having to worry about anyone else. It's put me in a much better space to decide that I want a partner to share experiences with but only if it makes me as happy as I was when I was alone.

* ** *

I love sleeping alone and having the whole bed to myself.

* ** *

It took a while to change my perspective. I had to recognize that my own company had worth, was valuable, and that I was enough. It was madness to try to make something work when I could tell in my heart of hearts that these suitors were not for me. I promised myself in my early thirties that I would no longer try to adjust who I was, my interests, or my standards in the pursuit of finding true love. I am a total romantic. I believe in finding a connection again with someone who is deep, loving, supportive, and shares my standards. Our culture perpetuates the toxic idea that a person's worth is measured by their romantic status, but we each have our own path to create and if we choose to share that with romantic partners, good for us.

***

I'm free to define my own worth.

***

I felt strong, raw, and awake to life. It was so freeing to have my living space all to myself and to be able to make decisions about what to do, where to put things, what music to listen to, what to eat, etc., without having to pause to consider the needs or wants of another person. And silence! It was so nice to have a lot of silence and stillness whenever I wanted. It never occurred to me how much I missed that or needed that until I got the chance to live alone.

***

Having me time with no one else to consider. Selfish? Yes. Wonderful? Yes.

It's good to be free, but I don't like it.

I think we're conditioned by society to think that finding someone to do life with is the equivalent of happiness, and we've never been taught to regard being single as something one could enjoy. Once I abandoned the fear of "ending up alone in life," I enjoyed spending time with myself.

***

Having 100 percent of my brain only dedicated to me instead of a relationship has been 💯.

***

I prefer to be in a partnership. I don't think of the single periods of my life with fondness. I spent most of the time I was single either trying to meet someone new, drinking very heavily, or both. I never really settled into being single in a healthy way.

***

I gained back so much of the confidence I had lost in my relationship.

***

I love the possibility. You never know when you might meet the love of your life.

***

I love being in a space where I can focus wholly on my own mental health.

***

It was scary for me when I was single, because I had been cou-pled for so long. I felt lonely, aimless, purposeless—bored. But feeling that way actually pushed me to dig into projects that I wanted to do just for me, and I ended up loving that aspect of being single. I had to construct every day from scratch, and to do that, I had to invent myself.

I can absorb just being me.

I have the dog all to myself!

It surprised me how much time I suddenly had when I was single! And how much time was left for reading the books I wanted to read, exercising, going to exhibits, or just being.

When I am single, I feel so much more rested.

I love being single and not having to fight with anyone!

Sooooo much less anxiety being single.

GRIEF HAS NO SCHEDULE...

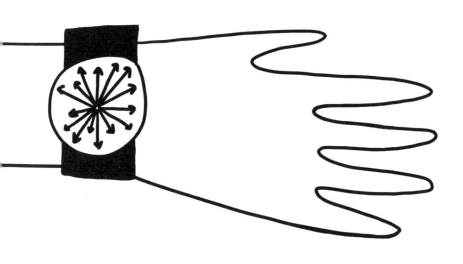

IT SHOWS UP
WHENEVER,
WITHOUT WARNING
OR INVITATION.

ANOTHER SPOT IN
THE MIDDLE

WHY IS THIS TAKING SOOOOO LONG?

BECAUSE GRIEF CAN RESEMBLE
THE OCEAN, GOING ON & ON, UP
& DOWN, CHANGING & EVOLVING
FROM ONE MOMENT TO THE NEXT.

EMOTIONAL CHECK-IN

check all the feels going on inside right now...

- ☐ SHOCK
- ☐ HOPE
- ☐ RAGE
- ☐ SADNESS
- ☐ RESENTMENT
- ☐ RELIEF
- ☐ HUNGER
- ☐ NUMBNESS
- ☐ EMPTINESS
- ☐ EXHAUSTION
- ☐ JEALOUSY
- ☐ GRUMPINESS
- ☐ APATHY
- ☐ _____
- ☐ _____
- ☐ _____

POSSIBLE ACTIONS TO FOCUS ON

- [ ] PUT ONE FOOT IN FRONT OF THE OTHER
- [ ] FUCK MAKING YOUR BED, JUST GET OUT OF IT IF YOU CAN
- [ ] GET DRESSED (SOMETIMES PAJAMAS ARE OKAY TOO)
- [ ] CONNECT WITH FRIENDS
- [ ] GET OUT OF YOUR HEAD
- [ ] LET'S BE HONEST, MAYBE MAKE OUT WITH SOMEONE?
- [ ] _____
  _____
  _____
- [ ] _____
  _____
  _____

LOCATE YOUR HEARTBREAK IN YOUR BODY

MARK ANY TENSE SPOTS,
POINTS OF JOY,
ACHES, CRAVINGS,
CRAMPS,
TENDERNESS,
OR WHATEVER
GRABS YOU.

DATING EVALUATION

ARE YOU READY TO DATE?
THE CLASSIC EQUATION WAS:
IT SHOULD TAKE 6 MONTHS FOR
EVERY YEAR SPENT TOGETHER TO
BE READY TO DATE AGAIN.

$$\frac{\text{total \# of years in relationship}}{\text{arbitrary amount of time}} \times 6 \text{ MONTHS} =$$

BULLSHIT. IF THIS IS HELPFUL
FOR YOU, GREAT. OUR JOB IS DONE.

IF NOT, NOTICE HOW YOU FEEL
ANSWERING THE FOLLOWING:

I AM...
- [ ] UNINTERESTED IN DATING
- [ ] COMPARING EVERYONE TO MY EX
- [ ] DAYDREAMING ABOUT US
- [ ] FANTASIZING THAT THINGS WORK OUT
- [ ] STILL HURTING
- [ ] GETTING A RUSH WHEN I SEE MY EX
- [ ] EXCITED TO MEET PEOPLE
- [ ] INTERESTED IN NEW EXPERIENCES
- [ ] AT PEACE
- [ ] READY TO LET GO OF THEIR STUFF

→ YOU MIGHT NEED MORE TIME. OR NOT? TRUST YOUR GUT.

→ NOW MIGHT BE A GOOD TIME TO TRY OUT THAT THING YOU'VE BEEN LONGING TO DO...

IT'S OKAY TO BE WHEREVER YOU'RE AT.

GRIEF PIE CHART

GRIEF CAN SOMETIMES PRESENT
ITSELF THROUGH A DIFFERENT EMOTION.

MARK WHERE YOU ARE RIGHT NOW:

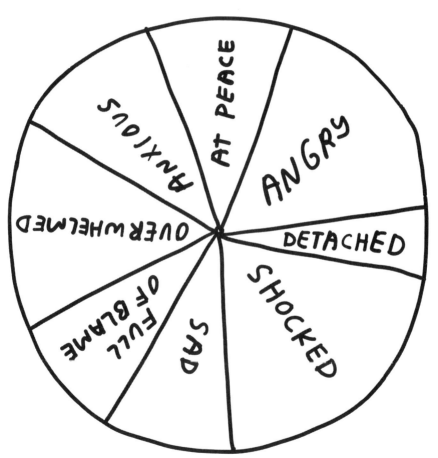

I AM GRIEVING.
IT FEELS LIKE:

REGRETS

MAKE A LIST OF THINGS YOU REGRET.

NOW THINK ABOUT WHICH REGRETS ARE
ACTUALLY HELPFUL TO YOU. DID THEY
HELP YOU LEARN? IF NOT, CROSS THEM
OUT & TRY TO FORGET ABOUT THEM. KEEP
ONLY THE ONES THAT ARE USEFUL.
* NOT USEFUL: I LOVED TOO MUCH.
* USEFUL: I WAS TRYING TO REPLACE
   MY LAST LOVER.

REAPPRAISE YOUR CURRENT THOUGHT

WRITE DOWN WHATEVER YOU'RE THINKING.

<u>example</u> They were grouchy because they hate me.

REWRITE THE THOUGHT
IN A WAY THAT HAS
NOTHING TO DO WITH YOU.

<u>example</u>| They were grouchy
because they had a
hard day.

THERE'S NO SUCH THING AS BEING LEFT

IT TAKES TWO PEOPLE TO EXIST WITHIN A RELATIONSHIP. IF IT ISN'T WORKING FOR ONE OF YOU, MAYBE IT ISN'T WORKING.

THEIR DYSFUNCTION

THEIR DESIRE

MAKE A LIST OF ALL THE THINGS
THAT DIDN'T WORK FOR YOU BOTH.
FIND THE CONNECTIONS.

MY DYSFUNCTION

MY DESIRE

RECLAIM CONTROL

WHAT CAN YOU CONTROL IN YOUR LIFE? BRAINSTORM THINGS THAT ARE YOURS. OWN THEM.

* GET A NEW HAIRCUT
* BAKE SOMETHING DELICIOUS

PLAN A PERFECT DAY*

HOW WOULD YOU WAKE UP?

WHAT WOULD YOU DO
  FOR FUN?

HOW / WHEN WOULD
  YOU SLEEP?

*IT'S OKAY NOT TO KNOW,
JUST GIVE IT A SHOT

WRITE DOWN WHY YOU THINK THE BREAKUP HAPPENED

* THEY HATE ME, I HATE THEM

NOW TRY REFRAMING IT OBJECTIVELY

* WE ARE BOTH PEOPLE DOING
THE BEST WE CAN WITH WHAT
WE'VE GOT

REMEMBER YOUR ROOTS

JOT DOWN PEOPLE & EVENTS
THAT HAVE SHAPED YOU.

BORN ON:

MY PARENTS:

WHAT VALUES DID YOU LEARN FROM THESE PEOPLE & EVENTS?

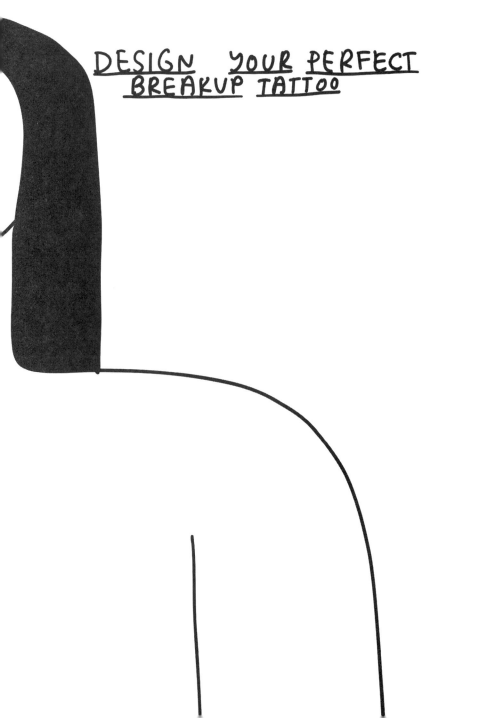

DESIGN YOUR PERFECT BREAKUP TATTOO

(the tattoo
Vera got.
Carissa was
there.)

WHAT MAKES YOU FEEL ATTRACTIVE?

DRAW YOURSELF LOOKING
SMOKING HOT (OR PASTE IN
A PHOTO OF YOURSELF THAT YOU LOVE)

THINKING ABOUT THE LONG TERM

WHERE WILL YOU BE SOON?

WHERE WILL YOU BE LATER?

WHERE DO YOU MOST WANT TO BE?

GRATITUDE SURVIVAL KIT

USE GRATITUDE AS A TOOL TO GET THROUGH HARD STUFF. WHEN YOU'RE DOWN, USE THIS KIT TO HELP LIFT YOU UP.

I'M GRATEFUL FOR...

- [ ]
- [ ]
- [ ]
- [ ]
- [ ]
- [ ]
- [ ]
- [ ]
- [ ]
- [ ]
- [ ]
- [ ]
- [ ]
- [ ]
- [ ]
- [ ]
- [ ]
- [ ]

AM I THE KEEPER OF OUR MEMORIES?*

WRITE OUT A MEMORY THAT WAS GOOD. MULL IT OVER IN YOUR MIND. YOU CAN STILL ENJOY IT. (IT'S STILL YOURS TO HOLD).**

* A REAL QUESTION VERA ASKED
(SHE HAD THE SOLE PHOTO ALBUM,
WITH TEN YEARS OF MEMORIES IN IT)
** BUT DON'T LET MEMORY CLOUD
YOUR JUDGMENT; THERE WERE
REASONS THINGS DIDN'T WORK OUT

DESCRIBE YOUR HEARTBREAK
MAKE IT CONCRETE SO YOU CAN KNOW IT BETTER.

COLOR:

SHAPE:

TASTE:

FEELING:

PAIN POINT:

MAYBE GIVE IT A NAME*
* 'SUP BRUNELLA

CELEBRATE ALL YOU'VE BEEN THROUGH
BY MEMORIALIZING IT HERE

Interlude

~~WEIRD~~
~~AWESOME~~
HOBBIES OF
THE NEWLY
SINGLE

SADNESS CAN BE <u>SUCH</u>
A GREAT MOTIVATOR

BAKING PASTRIES

BINGE-WATCHING TIKTOK

RENOVATING DOLLHOUSES

DOING PUZZLES

EATING SO MUCH CHOCOLATE

DRAWING

FLOSSING MY TEETH REGULARLY

DEADLIFTING AND SQUATTING

EATING SUSHI

KNITTING

WRITING POETRY

TAKING 5 A.M. WALKS (I WAS NEVER A MORNING PERSON BEFORE)

DONATING ALL THEIR OLD STUFF TO GIVE IT NEW LIFE

LISTENING TO LOUD MUSIC AS SOON AS I WAKE UP

WRITING LETTERS I WILL NEVER SEND

WORKING OUT TO ACHIEVE "REVENGE BUTT"

PLATE SPINNING

FENCING

PRACTICING BUTOH

MAKING OUT WITH STRANGERS

READING THREE-PLUS BOOKS A WEEK

GLASSBLOWING

KISSING MY OTHER EX

FLIRTING WITH MYSELF IN THE MIRROR

EATING WHILE STANDING UP IN THE KITCHEN

IT'S
BEEN
A LONG
TIME, BUT I STILL
DREAM ABOUT THIS
ONE EX. WE CATCH
UP. SOMETIMES WE
MAKE LOVE & I
WAKE UP LONGING.

PERMISSION TO WALLOW

YOU GOT THIS, EVEN IF YOU CAN'T GET OUT OF BED RIGHT NOW. SOMETIMES YOU NEED TO HEAL FROM HEARTBREAK IN A HORIZONTAL POSITION.

EMOTIONAL
CHECK-IN

check <u>all</u> the feels going
on inside right now...

- ☐ SHOCK
- ☐ HOPE
- ☐ RAGE
- ☐ SADNESS
- ☐ RESENTMENT
- ☐ RELIEF
- ☐ HUNGER
- ☐ NUMBNESS
- ☐ EMPTINESS
- ☐ EXHAUSTION
- ☐ JEALOUSY
- ☐ GRUMPINESS
- ☐ APATHY
- ☐ _____
- ☐ _____
- ☐ _____

POSSIBLE ACTIONS TO FOCUS ON

- ☐ PUT ONE FOOT IN FRONT OF THE OTHER
- ☐ FUCK MAKING YOUR BED, JUST GET OUT OF IT IF YOU CAN
- ☐ GET DRESSED (SOMETIMES PAJAMAS ARE OKAY TOO)
- ☐ CONNECT WITH FRIENDS
- ☐ GET OUT OF YOUR HEAD
- ☐ LET'S BE HONEST, MAYBE MAKE OUT WITH SOMEONE?
- ☐ _____
  _____
  _____
- ☐ _____
  _____
  _____

LOCATE YOUR HEARTBREAK IN YOUR BODY

MARK ANY TENSE SPOTS,
POINTS OF JOY,
ACHES, CRAVINGS,
CRAMPS,
TENDERNESS,
OR WHATEVER
GRABS YOU.

I LONG TO FEEL THIS AGAIN

* MAYBE THE THING YOU LONG FOR IS A FEELING AND NOT A SPECIFIC PERSON?

MAKE A PLAYLIST FOR WALLOWING

title

MOOD UNIFORM

DESIGN A DRESS CODE SO YOU
DON'T HAVE TO THINK SO MUCH.

WHEN I AM FEELING_____
I WANT TO WEAR_____
_____
_____

WHEN I AM FEELING_____
I WANT TO WEAR_____
_____
_____

WHEN I AM FEELING_____
I WANT TO WEAR_____
_____
_____

WHEN I AM FEELING_____
I WANT TO WEAR_____
_____
_____

ME LOOKING FINE AS HELL

DRAW OR WRITE WHAT THIS
FEELS LIKE TO YOU.

WRITE A MEMORIAL TO YOUR RELATIONSHIP

COUPONS FOR SELF-INDULGENCE

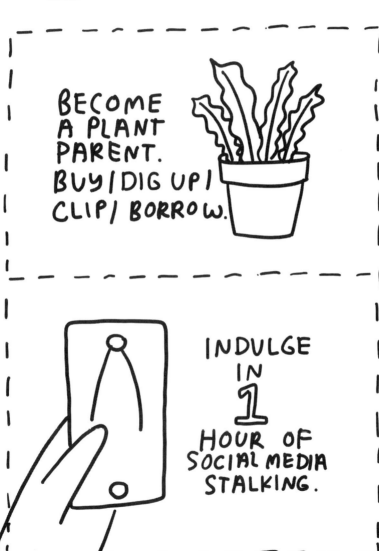

BECOME A PLANT PARENT. BUY/DIG UP/ CLIP/ BORROW.

INDULGE IN 1 HOUR OF SOCIAL MEDIA STALKING.

SHOW UP FOR YOURSELF.
LISTEN TO YOUR WANTS &
NEEDS. FOLLOW THEM.

NOW MAKE YOUR OWN

LICENSE TO:

_____

_____

EXTRAVAGANT IDEA:

_____

_____

PERMISSION TO:

_____

_____

INDULGE IN THE
THE LUXURY OF:

_____

_____

RITUALIZE YOUR GRIEF

THINK OF A SMALL ACTION
YOU COULD DO EVERY DAY
AND ADD AN INTENTION.
GIVE YOURSELF THE SPACE
TO BE PRESENT.

BAKE A CAKE

EAT ONE SLICE AT A TIME FOR A WEEK. RELISH THE DECADENCE.

VISIT
HOWTOHEALFROMHEARTBREAK.COM
FOR RECIPE SUGGESTIONS

A DAY WITHOUT "SHOULDS"

GIVE YOURSELF ONE DAY WITHOUT OBLIGATIONS. WHAT WOULD THAT LOOK LIKE? MAP OUT THE WHOLE DAY.

SOME (BITTER)SWEET MEMORIES

WRITE DOWN YOUR LAST GOOD
MEMORY OF THE PERSON.

WRITE DOWN YOUR LAST HARD
MEMORY.

WHAT DO YOU FEEL IN YOUR
BODY AS YOU REFLECT ON EACH
MEMORY?

OKAY, STAND UP & SHAKE IT OUT.

ALL THE PARTS OF ME YOU FOUND UNLOVABLE

- TOO NEEDY
- NOT ORGANIZED
- ALWAYS BURNT THE TOAST

(GIVE THOSE PARTS OF YOURSELF
A HUG.)

TIME / SPACE TRAVEL

PLAN YOUR IDEAL VACATION.
PLANNING CAN BE JUST AS
PLEASURABLE AS DOING !!!

LOCATION:

SEASON:

ACTIVITIES:

FRIENDS I WOULD SEE:

CLOTHES I WOULD WEAR:

MOVIE STAR I WOULD FEEL
 LIKE:

MEALS:

JUST LIE THE EFF DOWN, IT FEELS GOOD

LIE ON THE FLOOR & FEEL THE HARD SURFACE PRESSING INTO YOUR BODY.*

* ON THE ONE HAND, YOU'RE A MESS & YOU'RE ON THE FLOOR. ON THE OTHER, THE GROUND IS RISING UP & SUPPORTING YOU.

WALLOW IN A FICTIONAL ROMANCE

WRITE THE OPENING LINES OF A ROMANCE NOVEL THAT YOU WILL NEVER SHOW ANYBODY.

WRITE THE SEX SCENE YOU
WISH YOU WERE IN RIGHT NOW.

& MAKE TIME TO MASTURBATE.
IT'S FUN.

SERVE A CANDLELIT DINNER FOR ONE

SAVOR THE SUBLIME INDULGENCE
OF A ROMANTIC DINNER JUST FOR YOU.
WHAT ARE YOU CRAVING?
OUR IDEAL MEALS FOR ONE:
STEAK FRITES
CHEESY BAKED PASTA
ICE CREAM

VISIT
HOWTOHEALFROMHEARTBREAK.COM
FOR IDEAS

HOW DO YOU KNOW IF YOU'RE OVER IT?

SOME POSSIBILITIES FROM AN INFORMAL POLL ON INSTAGRAM

MAYBE THERE IS NO SUCH THING AS CLOSURE AFTER ALL?

You're over it when you:

* stop moving through the world hoping to see them.

* can think about them without a searing emotional response.

* can remember the good parts without wanting to go back to them.

* want the best for them.

* can get back to normal in only one day after having dreamt about them.

* just stop loving them.

* no longer long for them.

* can make peace with the loss.

* stop thinking about the what-ifs.

* don't feel heart-wrenching pain and longing.

* don't think about it 24/7.

* can feel the anger and sadness subside.

* are no longer actively grieving, every single day.

* can accept the ending of it.

* forget their birthday and it becomes just another day.

* don't feel their absence anymore.

* no longer push away new love.

* love and appreciate yourself more than the loss.

* start feeling excited about future love.

* see that they are just human too.

* have let yourself feel all the grief.

* forget.

Some other possibilities, from the same poll:

* ?????????????????????????

* I'm still figuring it out, and it's been two years.

* You don't ever really get over it.

* I guess it doesn't break your heart daily anymore, but I think we truly think about it forever.

* As someone not remotely healed yet, for me it's counting the days that I'm smiling.

* I hate the idea of being over someone.

* Love never goes away. And that hurts.

* I thought I knew the answer to this before I tried to answer the question.

* I wouldn't like not caring about my ex.

* You don't get over it, you just get used to carrying that specific sadness.

I AM AN EMOTIONAL BEING

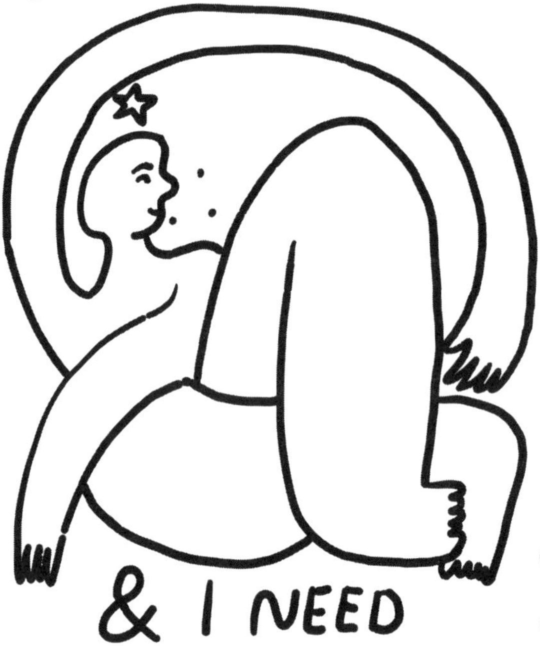

& I NEED TO HONOR THAT.

TOWARDS ACCEPTANCE

GETTING BY...
SORT OF

OR, HOW TO CONCLUDE SOMETHING*
THAT CAN'T REALLY CONCLUDE

* ALL THE PAIN & LOVE YOU'VE FELT

EMOTIONAL
CHECK-IN

check all the feels going
on inside right now...

- ☐ SHOCK
- ☐ HOPE
- ☐ RAGE
- ☐ SADNESS
- ☐ RESENTMENT
- ☐ RELIEF
- ☐ HUNGER
- ☐ NUMBNESS
- ☐ EMPTINESS
- ☐ EXHAUSTION
- ☐ JEALOUSY
- ☐ GRUMPINESS
- ☐ APATHY
- ☐ _____
- ☐ _____
- ☐ _____

POSSIBLE ACTIONS TO FOCUS ON

- [ ] PUT ONE FOOT IN FRONT OF THE OTHER
- [ ] FUCK MAKING YOUR BED, JUST GET OUT OF IT IF YOU CAN
- [ ] GET DRESSED (SOMETIMES PAJAMAS ARE OKAY TOO)
- [ ] CONNECT WITH FRIENDS
- [ ] GET OUT OF YOUR HEAD
- [ ] LET'S BE HONEST, MAYBE MAKE OUT WITH SOMEONE?
- [ ] _____
- [ ] _____

_____

_____

* COMPARE THESE PAGES TO THE FIRST CHECKLIST YOU DID. HAS ANYTHING SHIFTED FOR YOU?

LOCATE YOUR HEARTBREAK
IN YOUR BODY

MARK ANY TENSE SPOTS,
POINTS OF JOY,
ACHES, CRAVINGS,
CRAMPS,
TENDERNESS,
OR WHATEVER
GRABS YOU.

\# COMPARE
THIS BODY
MAP TO
THE FIRST
BODY MAP
YOU DID.
WHAT
HAS
SHIFTED?

DRAW OUT AN ENJOYABLE TIME YOU LIKE TO REMEMBER

DATE   /   /

WRITE ABOUT WHO
YOU WERE WITH, WHERE
YOU WERE, HOW IT FELT.

WHAT ADVICE WOULD YOU GIVE TO YOUR YOUNGER SELF?

PICTURE YOURSELF AT 80.
WHAT ARE YOU PROUD OF?
- I LOVED. & LOVED.

TRY LOOKING AT THE BIG PICTURE

FILL IN YOUR LIFE TIMELINE -
PAST, PRESENT, & FUTURE

birth   teens   20s   30s
|----------------|----------------|----------------|----------

40s   50s   60s

THIS MOMENT MAY FEEL
LIKE IT'S LASTING A LIFETIME,
BUT TRY PLACING IT IN THE
"BIG PICTURE."

MAKE A PLAYLIST FOR FEELING GOOD

title

THINGS I WANT TO DO
BUT PROBABLY SHOULDN'T

EXAMPLE/ EAT CAKE FOR ALL MEALS

EXAMPLE: EGG YOUR HOUSE

5 OLD FRIENDS

NAME 5 PEOPLE YOU WOULD WANT TO BE THERE FOR

1. _____

2. _____

3. _____

4. _____

5. _____

HAVE FAITH THAT THEY
WOULD WANT TO BE
THERE FOR YOU. REACH OUT.

5 THINGS I ~~LOVED~~ thought I LOVED ABOUT YOU

NOW REFRAME THEM AS NEGATIVES*:

*TRAITS CAN BE _BOTH_ POSITIVE
& NEGATIVE. SO MUCH IS
PERSPECTIVE.

NO ONE OWES ANYONE ANYTHING*

*FILE UNDER "THINGS MY THERAPIST SAID THAT STUNG AT THE TIME, BUT ACTUALLY MAKE SOME SENSE."

WRITE DOWN A FEW THINGS YOU
WISH YOU WERE OWED BUT AREN'T
- eternal devotion

A SPACE TO PUT ALL THE HARD QUESTIONS

WHAT IF I'M THE TOXIC ONE?

<u>NOW, A SPACE TO GIVE</u>
<u>YOURSELF</u> <u>LOVE & AFFECTION</u>

I BRUSH MY TEETH ON
THE REGULAR

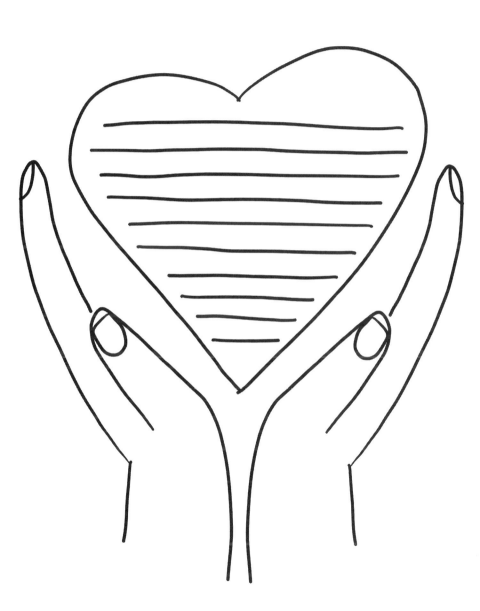

dear tiny me,

WHAT LESSONS WOULD
YOU SHARE?

dear present self,

WHAT ARE YOU LONGING
TO HEAR?

dear future self,

WHERE DO YOU HOPE
YOU WILL BE?

THE ~~CRUELTY~~ BEAUTY OF THE SUN
IT RISES & RISES & RISES.
WAKE UP EARLY ONE DAY WHEN
IT'S STILL DARK. LIGHT A CANDLE.
WAIT FOR THE SUN TO RISE.

a chance

to begin

again...

FIND AWE IN NATURE

LOOK OUT OVER A VAST
LANDSCAPE. NOTICE HOW
SMALL YOU ARE. WRITE
DOWN HOW YOU FEEL.

PART OF LIFE IS SWINGING
BETWEEN EMOTIONS. NOTICE
WHAT SURROUNDS YOU WHEN
YOU ARE FEELING:

HOPELESS

HOPEFUL

TAKE A SELFIE IN YOUR BATHROOM MIRROR

FOCUS ON THE THINGS YOU LOVE ABOUT WHAT YOU SEE. DO THIS LONG ENOUGH TO FEEL HOW MIRACULOUSLY BEAUTIFUL YOU ARE.

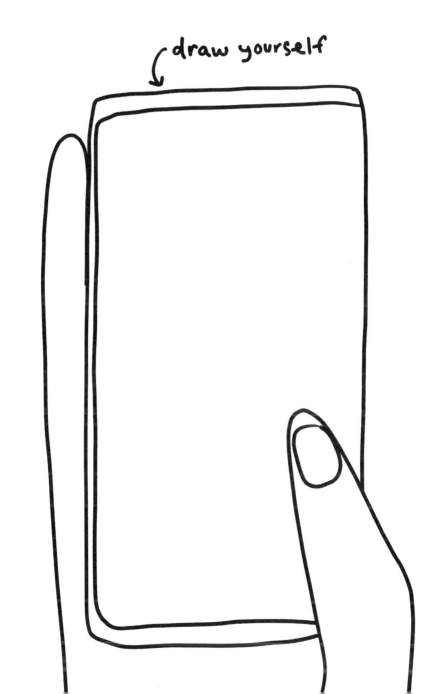

draw yourself

WHAT IS YOUR SUBCONSCIOUS TRYING TO TELL YOU?

WHAT HAVE YOU BEEN DREAMING ABOUT? IS THERE SOMETHING YOU ARE AVOIDING? ARE THE ANSWERS HIDDEN UNDER THE SURFACE?

MAKE A LIST OF ALL THE GOOD
(OR JUST NOT TERRIBLE) EXPERIENCES
YOU HAVE HAD SINCE THE BREAKUP.
THIS IS PROOF THAT THINGS CAN BE
OKAY, OR AT LEAST THAT TIME WILL GO ON
& YOU WILL COLLECT MORE GOOD
EXPERIENCES AS YOU GO.

WHERE DOES THE LOVE GO?

SOME THOUGHTS ON A CONCLUSION
THAT CAN NEVER REALLY CONCLUDE
(aka the myth of closure)

After a breakup, there's a question that always haunts us:

WHERE DID ALL THE LOVE I GAVE GO?

It is really painful to think that all of the love that was loved is just . . . gone.

But can this really be true?

After so many heartbreaks and a few lessons learned, our un-scientific but thoroughly researched and lived-through answer is: NO. One hundred million percent NO.

THE
LOVE
YOU
GAVE
WAS
NEVER
A WASTE.

The maddening, wildly beautiful, and truly painful thing about love is that there is seemingly no end to it. It's not a resource that can be measured in a cup and spilled out like yesterday's milk. Your love—yes, it was *yours*—is actually an infinite pool. You get to dip into it whenever you want.

Yes, you've suffered. We know you have, and we love every ounce of your suffering self. But imagine this: the depth of your suffering can only ever match the depth of your love. And yeah, that freaking sucks. But also, on our better days we think: *How lucky are we?* We are the people who feel things deeply. Who make emotional messes and then forget to clean them up. Who fall hopelessly, madly, and passionately in love. We feel it in our bellies and we feel it so hard our teeth hurt and our jaws clench. We fall over and over again. We're going to keep falling.

If you've made it this far, you probably know by now that this book is not going to "fix" you, though hopefully it made you feel a little less alone. It is incredibly important that you know you didn't need to be fixed. And also, that grief knows no timeline. It doesn't ever really end; it just changes shape over time. We have had this experience with the deaths of loved ones and with more am-biguous losses too, like romantic heartbreak or the dissolution of a friendship. Sometimes grief rushes to your side disguised as a fond memory; sometimes it erupts as a sex dream filled with longing; sometimes it manifests as a lead blanket weighing you down so hard that you just cannot get up. Sometimes it feels like . . . nothing at all.

It's okay to zoom in and out of your grief. To get to know it better. Give yourself permission to wallow and give yourself days off too. Force yourself to get out of bed and put clothes on, even though that takes every ounce of strength that you didn't know you had. If you just can't some days, text a friend. Ask them to help you. (People want to help.)

You have made it through some tough shit. And even though it doesn't feel this way right now, you did something beautiful: you loved & loved & loved & loved.

You will love again.

With all our (hopelessly broken,* endlessly romantic, stupid deadbeat) hearts,

VERA & CARISSA

---

* Somewhat less

NOTES

SPACE TO EXPLORE IT ALL.

NOTES

SPACE TO EXPLORE IT ALL.

RESOURCES AND FURTHER READING

There is absolutely no reason you have to hurt alone. Here are some resources.

BOOKS

A few of the places we've turned to for wisdom about heartbreak and grief.

W. H. Auden's poem "The More Loving One"

Pema Chödrön's *When Things Fall Apart*

Junot Diaz's *This Is How You Lose Her*

Joan Didion's *The Year of Magical Thinking*

Glennon Doyle's *Untamed*

Nora Ephron's *Heartburn*

Elena Ferrante's *The Days of Abandonment*

Jonathan Safran Foer's *Everything Is Illuminated*

Lori Gottlieb's *Maybe You Should Talk to Someone*

Sue Johnson's *Hold Me Tight*

Miranda July's *No One Belongs Here More Than You*

Rupi Kaur's *Milk and Honey*

Donika Kelly's poem "In the Chapel of St. Mary's"

Milan Kundera's *The Unbearable Lightness of Being*

Amir Levine and Rachel S. F. Heller's *Attached*

Thomas Lewis, Fari Amini, and Richard Lannon's *A General Theory of Love*

Gabriel García Márquez's *Love in the Time of Cholera*

Jenny Offill's *Department of Speculation*

Max Porter's *Grief Is the Thing with Feathers*

Sally Rooney's *Beautiful World, Where Are You*

Anna Sale's *Let's Talk About Hard Things*

Michelle Zauner's *Crying in H Mart*

MENTAL HEALTH RESOURCES

American Psychological Association psychologist locator: locator.apa.org

BetterHelp online therapy: betterhelp.com

Crisis Text Line: Text HOME to 741741 for anonymous, free 24/7 crisis counseling

National Domestic Violence Hotline: 1-800-799-SAFE (7233) or text START to 88788

National Institute of Mental Health: nimh.nih.gov/health/find-help

National Suicide Prevention Lifeline: 1-800-273-TALK (8255)

Psychology Today Find a Therapist: psychologytoday.com/us/therapists

RAINN's National Sexual Assault Telephone Hotline: 1-800-656-HOPE (4673)

Substance Abuse and Mental Health Services Administration (SAMHSA): findtreatment.gov

The Trevor Project: thetrevorproject.org/get-help, or reach their suicide prevention and crisis intervention hotline at 1-866-488-7386

Trans Lifeline's Hotline: 1-877-565-8860

Find links to these resources and more on howtohealfromheartbreak.com.

THANK YOU

We are indebted to so many people over the course of our lives for showing us the value of heartbreak and the meaning of love.

Thank you to our friends and family who have been with us through heartbreaks big and small, held us when we cried, left notes in our sock drawers to remind us of their love, and just generally fought to pick up the pieces and remind us of the beauty in the everyday. Your love is the love we've been waiting for.

Thank you to the dear friends and anonymous contributors who sent us stories for our interludes and guided us through the meaning of heartbreak. You've helped us (and others) feel less alone in the world.

We would like to thank each other. Carissa was the first person to hold Vera's newborn baby. Vera brought Carissa dinner every night when she lost hope. We wrote this book about the ending of romantic love but all along there was another love story cooking: the love between two friends.

Writing a book is a team effort and we would like to thank a few of the brilliant people who made it possible. To our agent, Nicole Tourtelot, thanks for seeing the potential in our idea and making every business conversation feel like a chat among friends. And to our editor, Lauren Appleton, who never went through a bad breakup but wanted to create a resource for her friends who were suffering, thanks for bringing our vision to life and for believing in us.

Lastly, we want to thank everyone out there who is holding it together enough to have the faith to get through a breakup. Your resilience is an act of grace.

Love,

VERA & CARISSA